ONTA

This edition published by W H Smith Publishers, Canada.

Produced by
Bison Books Corp.
15 Sherwood Place
Greenwich, CT 06830

Copyright © 1987 Bison Books Corp.

ISBN 0999936859

Printed in Hong Kong

INTRODUCTION

The province of Ontario is Canada's heartland. It lies in the middle of that vast country with its western boundary on the plains of Manitoba and its eastern point 1000 miles away on the broad St Lawrence River. Its northern reaches surround the subarctic Hudson and James Bays, and its southern border runs along four of the Great Lakes and the states of Minnesota, Michigan and New York.

The name Ontario is thought to derive from an Iroquois Indian word meaning 'the shining waters,' and nothing can better describe the province. Her shining waters include 68,490 square miles of freshwater ponds, lakes, rivers and streams as well as the many man-made canals and waterways that thread through the province.

About 10,000 years ago, at the end of the last ice age, the great glaciers which had covered most of North America retreated, leaving the Precambrian rock, now known as the Canadian Shield, exposed. The action of the ice and rocks also had dug great pits and holes of all sizes in the surface of the rock. These gradually filled with water to become the many lakes and ponds of Ontario. In the South, the rock eventually was covered by a deep layer of sediment which became the rich farmland of the Niagara peninsula and the Golden Horseshoe near Toronto.

The very size of the province is one of the reasons for the wide diversity in Ontario's climate. The cold of northern Ontario is tempered by the Great Lakes, and the province extends south to a point approximately on the same latitude as Boston, Massachusetts.

The hub of Canada, Ontario leads the rest of the country in population (one out of every three Canadians lives in Ontario) and per capita income. Renowned for its great industrial capacity, it is also a land rich in forests and farms, as well as the vast mineral wealth of the North, and the great hydroelectric schemes and commercial transport systems of the St Lawrence Seaway and the Great Lakes. It is the site of Canada's second largest city, Toronto (Montreal in the province of Quebec is the largest), which is also Canada's industrial, financial and intellectual capital. The large population sends 85 of the 265 members to the Canadian House of Commons in the federal capital of Ottawa, which lies within the province of Ontario.

The original inhabitants of the province were Indians, Inuit and Eskimo in the Far North, and members of either the nomadic Algonquin nation—the Cree, Ottawa and Mississauga tribes—or the woodland longhouse people of the Iroquois Confederacy—the Hurons and the Petuns. The first French explorers, Etienne Brule and Samuel de Champlain, reached the lands that would be Ontario in the early decades of the seventeenth century, and were soon followed by missionaries and traders. The Jesuits established a mission on Georgian Bay as early as 1639. The French influence lasted until all of Canada was ceded to Great Britain under the Treaty of Paris in 1763, which marked the end of the French and Indian War.

Ontario owes its provincial British heritage—distinct from Quebec's French heritage—primarily to those refugees from the newly established United States following the American Revolution, who are now known as United Empire Loyalists. With the influx of these colonists, the settlements on the Niagara peninsula and the Great Lakes shoreline developed a distinctly pro-British attitude. In 1791 Canada was divided into two colonies; Lower Canada, formally Quebec, so-called for its location on the lower end of the St Lawrence, closer to the mouth of the great river, and Upper Canada, the new English settlements upriver. The War of 1812 against the United States saw many skirmishes and battles in Upper Canada, including the burning of York (Toronto) and Niagara. There were naval engagements on Lakes Erie and Ontario as well. The many historic forts and battlefields testify to this era in Canada's past, which fostered a sense of unity and nationhood in the growing colony.

Immigration after the war brought more settlers of English, Scots and Irish descent to Upper Canada. By 1837 their number had increased the population by over one million, many of whom felt they deserved a voice in their own government and resented the power held by those earlier settlers of English descent who were by this time so intermarried and connected that they were known as the Family Compact. The more radical of the newer Canadians, led by a Toronto lawyer, William Lyon MacKenzie, actually revolted against the Family Compact. Their rebellion was unsuccessful, but their dissatisfaction did bring about a change in government by 1841. By the 1830s, Ontario had also become a terminus of the Underground Railroad, a refuge for escaped slaves from the southern United States. Many black families settled within the province.

The two colonies of Upper and Lower Canada were united, but the clash of English and French cultures continued. This division was somewhat alleviated at the time of Confederation in 1867, when Upper Canada and Lower Canada were again divided. Lower Canada once again became Quebec, and Upper Canada, which had become Canada West in 1861, had its name changed to Ontario.

Following Confederation, the transcontinental railroad, completed in 1885, brought the lands of the Far West closer to the more established parts of Canada and allowed settlement of the interior of Ontario by another wave of immigrants, including many from southern and eastern Europe. Among them were the German Mennonites who settled around Kitchener (then called

Berlin) and Waterloo. The area of the province reached the boundaries it maintains today in 1912 when the northern region along Hudson Bay was annexed from the Northwest Territories.

Since that time, the province has continued to develop, offering land and work to millions from all over the world. Despite the continued importance of her traditional industries—farming, commercial fishing and lumbering—Ontario today is the most urbanized of the Canadian provinces, with cities like Ottawa, Toronto, Kingston, Windsor and Thunder Bay. Her real wealth lies outside her cities, however, not only with the vast mineral resources of the North, near Sudbury, but also in the extraordinary range of National and Provincial Parks—from the marshy birdwatchers' paradise of Point Pelee, which reaches into Lake Erie, to the frozen treeless tundra of Polar Bear Provincial Park on the shore of Hudson Bay, which is accessible only by small plane.

The vast and diverse land that is Ontario encompasses pleasing extremes—from the cosmopolitan city of Toronto to the primitive and fertile Mennonite farms of Waterloo County, and from the barren landscape of the North near Sudbury to the thousand lakes of Kenora. Ontario and her people have been described as a mosiac, each different piece adding to the beauty and harmony that is the whole.

NIAGARA

Niagara Falls is, without question, one of the natural wonders of the world. More than 5300 feet wide in total and over 160 feet high, the two cataracts carry 500,000 tons of water over the rim of the falls every minute. The falls have been an attraction since their discovery by the Belgian priest, Father Jean-Louis Hennepin, in 1678. Hennepin described them as 'a vast and prodigious Cadence of Water,' and nothing in the 300 years since has diminished the grandeur of his statement.

The Falls at Niagara are not the highest in the world—that honor belongs to Victoria Falls in Zimbabwe— and they are only half as wide as Iguazu Falls on the border of Brazil and Argentina in South America. Like Iguazu, Niagara Falls lies on an international boundary, since the Niagara River forms the border between the United States and Canada. Niagara Falls may well be the world's most popular, as more than fourteen million people visit the Falls each year to view this wonder from a score of lookouts on either side of the river. Many people think of the Canadian or Horseshoe Falls when they think of Niagara, for their size and curved shape give them the more dramatic appearance. Also 95 percent of the water cascades over the Falls on the Canadian side, frequently obscuring them in the rising mist. This volume of water has created a great pool at the foot of the Falls which contrasts to the several tons of rock that have fallen from the lip of the falls on the American side and still lie at the base of the cataract.

At the time of Hennepin's discovery, the curve of Horseshoe Falls was very shallow, and the noise of the Falls could be heard as far away as Lake Ontario, 20 miles downstream. It is believed that the Falls themselves, which were created following the retreat of the glaciers only 10,000 years ago, were originally placed in the vicinity of Queenston 10 miles north of their current location, and gradual erosion has brought them halfway down the Niagara River between the two cities of Niagara Falls.

Both the American and the Canadian cities have established parks beside the river. The Canadian one, known as Queen Victoria Falls park, was the first Canadian Provincial Park, founded in 1887. Other views of the Falls are available from the cable car that travels low over the whirlpool and gorge; and from the damp but exhilarating voyage into the spume at the base of the Falls aboard the small steamer, *Maid Of The Mist*. It is also possible to walk behind the Falls through a series of tunnels, caves and platforms if the visitor is properly raincoated.

At the north end of the Niagara Parkway lies the charming village of Niagara-on-the-Lake, situated where the river flows into Lake Ontario. Rebuilt in 1813 after its capture and burning by the American forces in the War of 1812, the town, once the administrative center of Upper Canada, is today considered one of the best preserved nineteenth-century communities in North America. Niagara-on-the-Lake is also home to the famous summer Shaw Festival and the Canadian Mime Theatre.

But it is Niagara Falls that is the great attraction of the area. A popular destination for honeymooners since the nineteenth century, Niagara Falls still has the extraordinary ability to impress its visitors whether the great torrents boil over the lip of the cataract in the warmer months or are caught, frozen and gleaming, in the winter sun.

15 The tourist boat, Maid Of The Mist, *brings raincoated visitors to the foot of Niagara Falls.*

16 A gaily-painted Spanish cable car swings low over the gorge above the Niagara River whirlpool.

17 The most breath-taking view of this spectacular natural wonder can be seen at the very brink of the Canadian Falls at Table Rock.

18/19 The Canadian Falls at Niagara are almost 3000 feet across at their widest point, twice as wide as the American Falls.

20/21 The American and Canadian, or Horseshoe, Falls are separated by Goat Island which is in the United States.

22 The Niagara Apothecary in the charming village of Niagara-on-the-Lake has been in business since 1866.

23 The Prince of Wales Hotel, founded in 1854, is typical of the Victorian architecture that abounds in the Niagara Falls area.

24/25 There are many lookouts in the parks beside the Niagara River Gorge with wonderful views of the Falls.

OTTAWA AND THE ST LAWRENCE

Ottawa, from the Indian word meaning 'a place of buying and selling,' is situated perfectly for the capital of Canada, for it stands in the geographic center of the country, an English-speaking city across the river from the francophone city of Hull in Quebec. Originally the farm of Nicholas Sparks, after 1826 the settlement that would become Ottawa grew up around the excavations for the Rideau canal which was being built by the Royal Engineers under the direction of Colonel John By. The canal would allow British ships to come through to Lake Ontario from the St Lawrence but avoid the stretch which formed the United States' border. By 1832 the canal was complete, with a series of eight locks to allow ships to travel from the level of the Ottawa River to the top of the bluff, and the settlement called Bytown in the Colonel's honor, had become a center for the lumber trade.

When the various provinces of the colony of Canada pressed for confederation in the nineteenth century, it was expected that one of the established cities would be considered for the capital. It was Queen Victoria herself who chose Bytown, which had changed its name to Ottawa in 1855, as the capital, ignoring older cities, such as Quebec, Montreal, Kingston and Toronto. Scathingly referred to by detractors as 'Westminster in the Wilderness,' the new capital began an intensive building program in 1859, modeling its government buildings after those of the English Parliament in London, and constructing them in a similar Gothic Revival style.

A city of parks and gardens, as well as the oldest arboretum (1826) in Canada, beautiful Ottawa stretches along either side of the Rideau Canal and up the bluff overlooking the river. The Gothic government buildings still dominate the skyline. Across the Rideau canal can be seen the fairy-tale turrets of the Chateau Laurier, the best-known hotel in the city. But many modern buildings have also sprung up, including the National Arts Centre, the City Hall and the Ottawa Civic Centre. In the spring, the gardens of Ottawa bloom with tulips and other bulbs which are a gift of thanks from the government of Holland for the hospitality given by Canada to the exiled Dutch Royal Family during World War II.

The Ottawa River flows east from the capital, meeting the St Lawrence within the boundaries of the province of Quebec. Upstream the St Lawrence becomes an international boundary between the State of New York and the Province of Ontario, passing many wildlife sanctuaries and historical sites. Where Lake Ontario flows into the river lies the vacationers' paradise known as the Thousand Islands. Local Indian legend says that the Great Spirit created a paradise in an attempt to bring peace to two warring tribes. When they resumed fighting, the Great Spirit gathered his paradise into a blanket which tore as he flew back to the heavens, and the paradise was broken into hundreds of pieces when it hit the earth. The many islands of various sizes have been a favorite summer resort of Americans and Canadians since the last century. The green islands in the changing blue of the St Lawrence still beckon vacationers, especially in the warm summer months, and when the leaves first begin to turn red, yellow and gold.

27 The 291-foot Peace Tower stands at the center of the government buildings of Ottawa's Parliament Hill.

28/29 The Gothic architecture of the Parliament buildings and the Chateau Laurier across the Rideau Canal is highlighted by an autumn sunset.

30/31 Ottawa's Rideau Canal is a skater's dream in winter. The National Arts Centre which stands beside the canal contains three theatres and is home to the National Arts Centre Orchestra.

32 The charming setting of the traffic-free Sparks Street Mall in the heart of Ottawa attracts many visitors.

33 An impressive steel-and-glass building designed by Arthur Erickson houses the Bank of Canada in Ottawa.

34 The tulips in the parks and gardens of Ottawa are a gift from the government of Holland to commemorate Canadian hospitality to the Dutch Royal Family in exile during World War II.

35 Fresh vegetables, flowers and cheese have been sold at Ottawa's Byward Market since 1846, before the establishment of the Canadian capital.

36 The Library, completed in 1878, with its 132-foot dome and rich paneling, was one of the few Parliament buildings untouched by the fire of 1916.

37 A summer attraction in Ottawa is a boat trip on the Rideau Canal, which has a rise of eight locks from the Ottawa River to the top of the bluff.

38/39 The skyline of Ottawa from Hull, Quebec, across the river shows the fairy-tale towers of the Chateau Laurier and the Parliament buildings on the other side of the Rideau Canal.

40 The 1000 Islands of the St Lawrence River that lie between Gananoque and Brockville are a famous summer resort, filled with cottages of all shapes and sizes.

41 Near Rockport on the St Lawrence is a popular harbour for cruisers and fishermen.

42/43 Some of the 1000 Islands are only large
enough to hold a small cabin and a dock.

44/45 Daily life in Canada between 1784 and 1867
can be seen near Morrisburg at Upper Canada
Village, a reconstructed town of period buildings
which had been threatened by the construction
of the St Lawrence Seaway.

TORONTO

The Indian word *toronto* is thought to mean a meeting place, and was used, soon after the first white men came to this part of Canada, to describe the place of portage between Lake Ontario and the Holland River. An Indian village called Teiaiagon, and later a French trading post and two forts, Rouille and Toronto, were built nearby. Following their victory in the French and Indian War, the British began negotiations for the purchase of that particular stretch of land from the Indians.

In 1793 the Governor of Upper Canada, John Graves Simcoe, who wanted to establish a seat of administration further away from the threat of possible American invasion than Niagara-on-the-Lake, chose the Indian village near the ruins of Fort Toronto and changed its name to York. Simcoe was proved correct when Niagara was attacked and burned during the War of 1812. Unfortunately York was also captured and destroyed during that campaign. When the rebuilt town was incorporated as the new provincial capital in 1834, the name was changed back to Toronto.

By the middle of the nineteenth century immigrants, especially those from the British Isles who made up the majority of Toronto's citizens, had brought the population of the city to over 40,000. These people brought a conservative attitude and outlook to the city that it would retain until refugees following World War II created an ethnic variety which served to transform the somewhat stolid city known as Toronto the Good into a more cosmopolitan and lively place.

Today, Toronto is a vibrant and engaging city which combines small neighborhoods, remarkable universities, great skyscrapers and a population of more than three million people who roots are spread all over the world. One out of every ten Canadians lives in Toronto. As well as being the provincial capital, Toronto has become the financial capital of Canada, with head offices of many of the country's chartered banks and the second largest stock exchange in North America. The city also enjoys great cultural wealth and diversity. The expanding skyline features many buildings of architectural importance, including the CN Tower, the world's tallest free-standing structure, and the New City Hall on Nathan Phillips Square. There are several fine universities in Toronto, and the museums and art galleries are as well-known as the Metro Toronto Zoo and the two distinct amusement parks, Wonderland and Ontario Place. A center for Canadian sports, Toronto is the home of a major-league baseball team and one of the great hockey teams. The cultural attractions of Toronto include theatre and music, especially the renowned Toronto Symphony. Over two hundred years after its establishment the city is still living up to its name—the meeting place.

47 Toronto's CN Tower, a broadcast and receiving station, also contains restaurants and observation decks. At 1815 feet, it is the tallest free-standing structure in the world.

48/49 Toronto has become a cosmopolitan city of modern architecture, restful plazas and pocket parks.

50/51 The Toronto Harbour islands provide a magnificent view of the expanding city skyline.

52 Among the popular attractions at Canada's Wonderland, near Toronto, is the fabulous roller-coaster.

53 Ontario Place, in Toronto's harbour, features
cafes, theatres and water amusements such as
pedal boats as well as the Cinesphere where films
are shown on a curved screen.

54 The new City Hall on Nathan Phillips Square, a pair of curved towers surrounding the domed city council chambers, was designed by Viljo Revell and completed in 1965.

55 The Eaton Centre is an enormous shopping complex, stretching from Dundas to Queen Street, containing three levels of shops and restaurants.

56 *One of the world's greatest hockey teams, the Toronto Maple Leafs have won the Stanley Cup 11 times.*

57 top *The Toronto Blue Jays is the only Canadian baseball team in the American League. The club joined the league in 1977.*

57 bottom *The Molson Grand Prix was run for the first time in Toronto in August 1986.*

58 Chinatown, one of Toronto's many ethnic neighborhoods, has wonderful shops and restaurants.

59 Caribana, a weekend festival in July, celebrates the ethnic heritage of Toronto's many West Indians.

60 *The St Lawrence market on Front Street, open every weekend, has been a farmers' market since 1815.*

61 Kensington Market opened as a strictly Jewish market, but now caters to all the city's ethnic minorities.

62 *The Royal Alexandra Theatre, founded in 1907, has been lovingly restored as a legitimate theatre for touring plays and musicals.*

63 Roy Thomson Hall on King Street is the new home of the famed Toronto Symphony Orchestra.

SOUTHERN ONTARIO

The 'shining waters' that gave the province of Ontario her name are most obvious in the southern triangle, the area west of Toronto and the Niagara peninsula, which is almost surrounded by the Great Lakes. This is also the part of Ontario and indeed of Canada that is the most populous, for here also lie the cities of Hamilton, at the western end of Lake Ontario, Sarnia at the bottom tip of Lake Huron, and Windsor, across the Detroit River from the American city of that name.

East of Lake Huron lies the rich farmland of the province, which includes those farms owned and run by the Mennonites, members of a sect who fled to North America from Europe in the middle of the seventeenth century, and still keep to their ancient way of life. The first group came to Canada in 1784, and settled generally in the area around Kitchener and Waterloo. Like their kinsmen in the United States, the Canadian Mennonites speak their own language—Pennsylvania Dutch—and run their enormous farms by horsepower and time-honored agricultural skills. The richness of these farms is obvious in the abundance of crops and the health of the stock. Many Mennonite women earn pin money by selling cheese, baked goods, sausage and handicrafts at roadside stands or at the weekly farmers' markets in Elmira, Waterloo and Kitchener.

Kitchener is also famous for the Oktoberfest, a nine-day celebration of German food, drink and music, in honor of the city's heritage. Settled by Germans in 1833, Kitchener was called Berlin until World War I.

The southernmost point in Canada is the National Park at Point Pelee, which enjoys the longest frost-free growing period in the country, for it lies on Lake Erie. The marshland has become a extraordinary wildlife refuge, a paradise for birdwatchers, but is best-known as one of the major migratory rests for the monarch butterflies, who pause there each September in their thousands, before resuming the flight to their winter homelands in Central America.

At the northwest end of Southern Ontario lies the Bruce Peninsula, which separates Lake Huron and Georgian Bay. This is part of the rocky spine which stretches from Lake Ontario to Manitoulin Island in the North and is a favorite place for vacations. It is well-known for the number of shipwrecks which attract skin divers and for the extraordinary limestone formations, cliffs and caves. Nearby in Midland is a reconstruction of Sainte-Marie among the Hurons, one of the earliest French missions to the Indians. The original was built by the Jesuit Jean de Brebeuf, who was martyred there with five other priests in 1639. Brebeuf and his followers are honored at the nearby Martyrs' Shrine which has become a place of pilgrimage. At Midland, the gentle rolling farmland begins to give way to the forest and rocky tracts that are the North.

65 The Grand River flows past the stone buildings on Mill Street in the town of Elora.

66/67 The rolling countryside near Creemore in Simcoe County is typical of the rich farmland in southern Ontario.

68 *The Stratford Shakesperean Festival, which begin in a tent in 1953, now has three theatres and includes the works of other playwrights in its repertoire.*

69 *Swans on the River Avon in Stratford entertain theatregoers and tourists alike.*

70/71 The Peterborough Lift Lock at Lock 21 on the Trent-Severn Waterway dates from 1904 and is the largest hydraulic lift lock in the world.

72/73 The lighthouse at Point Abino on Lake Erie guides ships leaving or approaching Buffalo, New York or the Welland Canal.

74 The boardwalk at Point Pelee National Park, a wildlife refuge teeming with rare plants and animals, brings visitors to a wooden observation tower in the middle of the park's marsh.

75 Point Pelee, the southernmost point on the Canadian mainland, is one of the migratory rests for the monarch butterfly and thousands of them can be sighted there each autumn.

76/77 One of the locks on the Trent and Severn waterway, which connects Trenton on Lake Ontario with Georgian Bay, is found at Lindsay.

DANGER
UNDERTOW

NO BOATING
NO SWIMMING

RESSAC DANGEREUX
EMBARCATIONS
ET
BAIGNADE INTERDITES

78/79 The steel city of Hamilton on the shores of Lake Ontario is also known for its beautiful gardens.

80 Sainte-Marie among the Hurons is a painstaking reconstruction of the early settlement which includes a seventeenth-century chapel. The Martyrs' Shrine is nearby.

81 Mennonite women gather outside a meeting house near Waterloo.

82 The Mennonites are great farmers and sell extra produce, cheese and sausage at farmers' markets and roadside stands.

83 Only the warning traffic triangles reveal that this scene of tethered Mennonite buggies outside the meeting house in West Montrose is modern.

84 Oktoberfest in Kitchener is celebrated with parades, German bands, dancing and vast quantities of food and drink.

85 Highland dancers perform a reel outside Dundurn Castle near Hamilton.

THE NORTH

In the early twentieth century, the writer and naturalist known as 'Grey Owl' described northern Ontario as 'a great lonely land of forest, lake and river where moose, deer, bears and wolves run free.' Little has happened to invalidate that description. The lakes of northern Ontario are renowned as an anglers' paradise, for they provide fishermen hours of relaxation and pleasure in search of walleye, pike, *ouananiche* and trout. Hunters, also, pursue their sport in the proper season, in search of deer, moose and occasionally elk. Many of the great provincial parks of the north, like Quetico, Algonquin and Killarney, require the visitor to hike and canoe to reach their wilderness fastness. The Canada of the trappers and great fur trading companies is still alive in the North.

By contrast, the great cities of this area have changed the landscape to provide the riches they are famed for. Sudbury in the desolate region north of Georgian Bay is the center of Canada's mineral wealth, and her somewhat barren landscape is rich in nickel, copper and other ore. Thunder Bay on the shores of Lake Superior, the greatest of the Great Lakes, is the port for the great grain provinces of the prairies. Sault Sainte Marie, on the opposite side of Lake Superior, is one of the centers of the lumbering trade, as well as the second largest steel producing city (after Hamilton) in the province.

In contrast to southern Ontario, where man has certainly made an impression, with towns, cities and complicated systems of roads and canals, the North is isolated and unchanged. The few roads run for many miles within almost primeval forest between remote towns. One of the most remote towns is Cochrane, the terminus of the Ontario Northland Railway's train called the *Polar Bear Express*, which winds through 180 miles of marsh, muskeg and brush to the town of Moosonee on James Bay above the tree line. A canoe ride will bring the visitor to Moose Factory, Ontario's oldest fur trading post founded by the Hudson's Bay Company in 1673. Even further north, and accessible only by small plane, lies Polar Bear Provincial Park on the shores of Hudson Bay. The 9300 square miles of this subarctic park typify the region of low vegetation and abundant wildlife. Polar and black bears, Arctic fox and wolves, moose and caribou, and seals, as well as loons, Canada and snow geese and phalaropes, can all be found within the unusual reserve where the short balmy summer becomes harsh winter, and the rolling sea fog from Hudson Bay can cover the land.

87 The evening sun breaks through the clouds, illuminating the northern lakes.

88/89 The edge of Loon Lake near Haliburton is ringed with stumps of trees felled by fire.

90 A bull moose, one of the most sought-after game animals, moves through the autumn underbrush near Lake Superior.

91 Logs are floated down the Wabigoon River to the pulp mills at Dryden in the north woods of Ontario.

92/93 An ore freighter is gilded by the sunrise on Georgian Bay.

94/95 The Algoma Steel Company at Sault Sainte Marie, Ontario, has been manufacturing steel there since 1902.

96 Thunder Bay, at the western end of Lake Superior, is an important port for shipping grain and iron ore.

97 Lake Superior, seen from Thunder Bay, is the largest freshwater lake in the world.

98 A heavy parka with a fur-trimmed hood keeps a young Cree boy warm. Many of northern Ontario's citizens of members of Indian tribes.

99 The Ojibwa communities on Manitoulin Island hold festivals each summer, inviting other tribes to compete in dancing and sporting events.

100 Many of Ontario's lakes are so remote that fishermen must fly in to enjoy their favorite sport.

101 The SS Norisle, now retired to Manitowing on Manitoulin Island, carried passengers and vehicles from the island to Tobermory on the Bruce Peninsula.

102/103 The Ottawa River, near Deux Rivieres, is a popular location for the fast-growing sport of whitewater rafting.

104 A solitary canoist enjoys a morning paddle in Killarney Provincial Park, a wilderness on the north shore of Georgian Bay.

105 top The Ontario Northland Railway's Polar Bear Express from Cochrane is the only land access to Moosonee, a trading settlement on the shore of James Bay.

105 bottom The Big Nickel, which stands 30 feet tall, commemorates the mineral wealth of Sudbury, the center of the rich nickel and copper mining region.

106 *The Hudson's Bay Company's Staff House at Moose Factory, one of Ontario's earliest settlements, was founded in 1673.*

107 The town of Moosonee, situated above the tree line, is over 300 years old and contains a number of eighteenth-century structures.

l08/109 The polar bear is the king of the Canadian North.

GLIMPSES

Every place produces its own special atmosphere, for every place is unique. The many waves of people who settled Ontario brought with them a familiar way of building, of working, of living. The land then imposed upon these settlers its own restraints created by climate, geology and season. Together they created the character that gives Ontario its identity.

Each province of Canada has qualities that are well-known and recognizable, although some may be more obvious than others. The distinct quality of Quebec, for example, asserts itself in the language difference which still influences the province. Although the Atlantic Provinces share a maritime heritage, the distinct French, Scottish and Irish background of her settlers distinguish regions within each province, as well as one province from another. The broad prairie provinces each have their own essence. Ontario, as befits the province of the capital, lying in the center of the country, unifies the representative images of Canada's provinces in a heritage and landscape that presents itself, however fleetingly, in a series of glimpses.

Ontario cherishes her Loyalist heritage, the limestone houses and the battlefields of her eastern region, the many life-giving waterways, and the barren, treeless terrain of her northern country. She also values the impact of her later settlers, the German farmers near Waterloo, the Chinese that have enlivened her cities, and the native cultures of her many Indian tribes. The diversity of Ontario has made the province a treasure house of images to remember and prize.

Each traveler in Ontario forms his own particular memories, like photographs taken with the mind's eye, that make the place real for him. The memory can be of something as simple as frost patterns on a window, or the smooth surface of the rocks on Lake Superior, the soft shine of the ancient brass work on a Canadian ferry crossing Georgian Bay or the intense dark of a summer night near Thunder Bay. The native of Ontario, too, retains special memories—a particular turn of a road beneath autumn leaves, a winter's skating on the Rideau Canal, the pattern of light on a building he has known his whole life—that will always remind him of home.

111 Raccoons are found throughout the timber regions of the province.

112/113 Upturned lifeboats line a winter beach near Toronto.

114 Cranberries still hold their colour after an early snow.

115 The growing popularity of Nordic or cross-country skiing is evident during the long Ontario winter.

116 A voyageur at the Fort William Restoration near Thunder Bay brings the days of the old fur traders to life.

117 Mennonite girls in braids also wear the traditional simple dresses without buttons.

118/119 Colorful wooden chairs welcome visitors to Grand Bend on Lake Huron.

120 Logs are penned by log booms after coming down river to the sawmills and pulping factories.

120

121 Largemouth bass are one of the most common fish found in the lakes of Ontario.

122 A view through the Romanesque pillars across the lawn at the University of Toronto.

123 The West Block of the government buildings on Parliament Hill in Ottawa glimpsed through a Gothic doorway.

*124 On Lake of Bays near Huntsville, a wooden
pier stands deserted in the summer sun.*

124

125 The salvaged hull of HMS Tecumseh is one of the exhibits at the Naval and Military Establishments near Penetaguishene.

126/127 Near Markham, a line of trees breaks through the morning mists of autumn.